Thimbles & Things

Handmade Treasures for All Who Love to Sew

Kumiko Sudo

Breckling Press

Library of Congress Cataloging-in-Publication Data

Sudo, Kumiko.
 Thimbles & Things : handmade treasures for all who love to sew / Kumiko
Sudo.
     pages cm
Summary: "*Thimbles & Things* collects together a dozen projects perfect for sewing enthusiasts. As well as a variety
of thimble designs, there are needle cases, a cute sewing cache, pin cushions, a sew-and-go kit, and more. Drawings
and instructions help new sewers stitch-by-stitch along the way! All are inspired by Japanese style—colorful, delicate,
intricately designed, and great as gifts for anyone who loves to sew"—Provided by publisher.

Thimbles & Things includes projects previously published in other books
by Kumiko Sudo: *Wagashi*, *Kokoro no Te*, and *Flower Origami*.

ISBN 978-1-933308-42-5 (paperback)
1. Sewing. 2. Sewing—Equipment and supplies. 3. Textile crafts. I.
Title. II. Title: Thimbles and things.

TT715.S83 2015
646.2--dc23

                    2015021987

This book was set in Guardi, Lichten and Agenda
Editorial direction by Anne Knudsen
Calligraphy by Kumiko Sudo
Design and production by High Tide Design
Cover and interior photographs by Sharon Hoogstraten
Technical drawings by Eliza Wheeler and Kandy Petersen

My heartfelt thanks to friends and students in Japan who have generously
shared their kimono fabrics.

Published by Breckling Press
283 N. Michigan St, Elmhurst, IL 60126

This compilation of sewing projects is based on previously published patterns
in *Flower Origami*, *Kokoro no Te*, and *Wagashi* by Kumiko Sudo.

Printed and bound in China

International Standard Book Number (ISBN 13): 978-1933308-42-5

Love for Sewing

I learned to sew as a very little girl. At first, I would watch my mother and my aunt, and as I got older they would help me create new projects of my own from their scraps of leftover fabrics. Since all the women in my life sewed, I liked to make them little gifts to help them keep their needles, threads, pins, and other accessories tidy and pretty.

For those of us who love to sew, there are few more beloved gifts to give or receive than a charming sewing kit or tote that will help us keep our needles, pins, threads, and scissors safe and close to hand. A beautifully made sewing kit, a pincushion, or even a simple thimble crafted from fabric reminds us of the person who gave it. It is a token through which we remember her love and the care she took to make it. What gift could be more personal or more endearing?

Kumiko Sudo

Contents

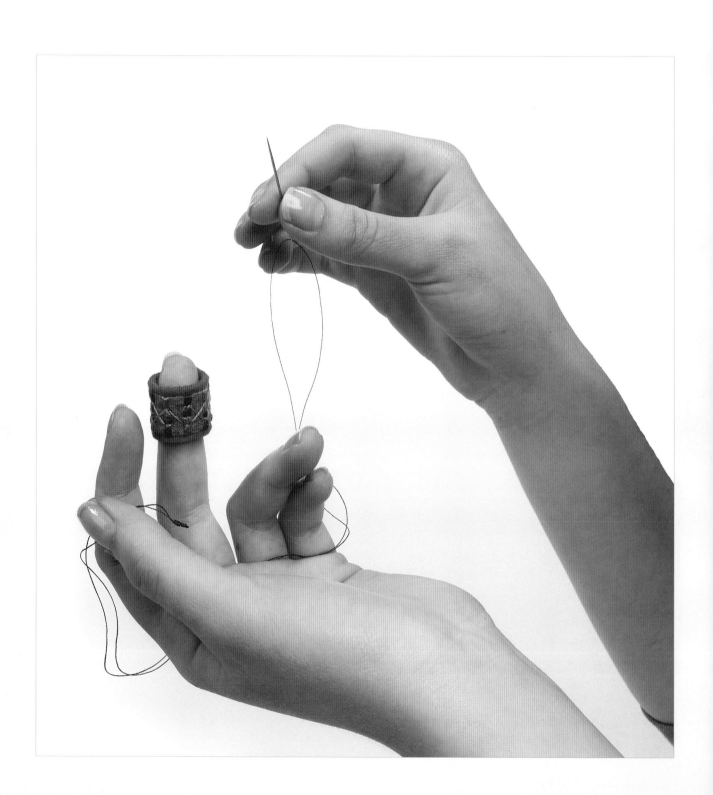

A Guide to Technique

In *Thimbles & Things*, you will find twelve projects. Some are very simple to make and perfect for sharing with beginners or even the youngest children. Others are a little more complex, but none is difficult. All can be made with simple hand-sewing skills. If you prefer to use a machine on the larger pieces, that is fine, too. Throughout my life, I have made sewing accessories like the ones in this book as gifts for my family and dearest friends. It is fun to pick out special little pieces of fabric and, within an hour or two, see a lovely new project take shape.

As you browse through this book, you will see that some projects incorporate familiar materials and techniques that I have used in my earlier collections. As before, I have chosen Japanese silks, American cottons, and soft, natural-woven felts to construct several of the items. Several projects include beading and embroidery. I encourage you to seek out unusual embellishments to add to your projects, making each gift you give unique and personal. Some of the projects are very simple and can be completed in less than an hour. *Bell Fruit Charms* on page 40 and, of course, my fabric

thimbles on page 18 are easy to make. Larger projects like the *Sun Rose Sewing Box* on page 22, which introduces fabric-origami flowers, can be completed in a day. Other projects, such as the more challenging *Tidy Tote* on page 52 or *Ivy Heart* on page 32 may take more time and patience, yet these are the ones that will give you the most pleasure, especially when you wrap them up as gifts for a special friend.

Fabrics

The projects in *Thimbles & Things* present you with a wonderful opportunity to showcase special fabrics. Many of the samples photographed are crafted from Japanese silks, shiboris, or chiromen crepe; other are made from beautifully designed and readily available contemporary cottons. For years, I have collected traditional Japanese textiles and I now have a large selection of antique kimono and obi. I have cut up several of them in order to incorporate their rich colors and patterns into my designs. I save each scrap, no matter how small, to make small gifts like the ones in this book.

To make the designs in *Thimbles & Things*, you do not need to have a large fabric collection, nor do you need to spend a lot of money. The projects are intended to be made from small scraps and you can easily mix and match fabrics within a single design. For this reason, I have not specified exact yardages for any of the projects. If you are shopping for new fabrics, I suggest you buy ⅛ yard of every fabric that catches your eye and ¼ yard of those that are irresistible. This way, you will have enough fabric for two, three, or more of the projects you are making. Look for a variety of colors and shades, and try to find some fabrics with strong motifs that you will be able to highlight in a pleasing way. Use the photographs as a guide to contrast, rather than trying to imitate my fabric choices. I suggest you select colors and patterns that you enjoy the most. It is the combinations you choose that will make your gifts unique.

Working with Felts

Many of the projects in *Thimbles & Things* incorporate felt. Soft to the touch, I particularly like to use felt as the lining for my sewing boxes and totes. Precious items like antique buttons or delicate beads slipped inside a felt-lined sewing cache remain safe and scratch-free. Quality felts are available by the yard from several companies. I particularly like the all-natural wool felts from National Nonwovens. They come in rich textures and a variety of luxurious colors. Avoid pre-cut craft felts, which are usually rough to the touch and may bleed upon exposure to damp or perspiration.

Quality felt is a delight to sew. Since it doesn't fray, there is no need for hemming. It holds even the smallest stitches securely. Use matching-color thread and your stitches will sink into the felt and become invisible.

Cutting

Full-size templates are provided for any fabric pieces you need to cut that are not simple squares, circles, and rectangles. If you plan on making several of the projects in the book, for instance if you are making thimbles for everyone in your sewing circle, I recommend that you make templates of these basic shapes from template plastic or stiff card. This will save you the trouble of measuring and drawing new shapes each time you need one. See the next page for help on making templates.

Read the pattern and the template pieces carefully to make sure you allow the correct seam allowance for each piece. Most of the small projects here use ¼" or even ⅛" seam allowances. For circles, squares, and rectangles, the seam allowance is already included in the measurement provided.

Felt, used as lining or padding for several projects, requires no seam allowance at all. Since the templates are all quite small and multiples of the same piece are rarely needed, I use sharp scissors rather than rotary cutting equipment. Whichever method you use, remember to transfer any markings from the pattern onto the cut pieces of fabric.

Using Templates

All templates are drawn to full size and do not include seam allowances, unless specified otherwise. You will find that for many projects you will need to cut the same shape first from felt and then from fabric. Begin by tracing or photocopying the template onto template plastic or stiff card. Transfer all labels and markings. Using tailor's chalk or another quilters' marker, lightly draw around the template, then cut the felt pieces you need. Next, eyeball the correct seam allowance—usually ¼" or ⅛", as indicated on the template. Draw around the template, directly onto your fabric, adding that seam allowance in. If you are uncomfortable estimating the seam allowance, remake your templates on a new sheet of template plastic or card, this time with the seam allowance already added in. Remember that sewing is very forgiving—if your seam allowance is slightly off, it will not be noticeable on the finished piece.

Sewing

I sew everything —straight seams and curved seams, piecing and appliqué—by hand. When I sew, I feel my hands are directed by my heart and I like the sense of intimacy that handsewing gives me. I am particularly sensitive to this emotion when I am making gifts. Since all the projects in the book are quite small, you may want to sew them by hand, too. If you prefer to sew by machine, you will find that straight seams, such as the side seams in larger projects like

the sewing tote on page 52, turn out beautifully. In certain projects, however, where you may need to manipulate the fabric as you sew, you may find that handsewing is not only faster, but more accurate.

Some of the designs involve sewing curved seams. For perfect curved seams, I use a form of appliqué or invisible stitching that is described below. My technique involves placing a fabric piece, with the seam allowance folded under, on top of a background piece; the piece is then blind-stitched by hand. In the instructions, this is what is meant by the term *appliqué*. The term *sew* indicates a more traditional method of sewing the pieces together, right sides facing, using a running stitch on the wrong side of the seam lines. Straight seams are sewn in this way, and you may use hand or machine stitching.

Appliqué Stitches

The appliqué technique I use to attach appliqués of flowers, leaves, or stems onto my projects results in tiny stiches that are not visible from the front. The appliqués lie flat, for a smooth, clean effect.

1. Fold under the seam allowance of the appliqué (A) and press or finger-press it firmly. Pin the appliqué in place through the seam allowance onto the background fabric (B).

2. Insert the needle through a single thread in the weave of background fabric. As soon as it emerges from the fabric, re-insert the needle into the appliqué at the fold line. Exit at a point ¼" further along the fold line. This will neatly hide the knot in the folded seam allowance.

3. Repeat, pulling the thread firmly with each stich. In effect, the thread is hidden in the "tunnel" inside the folded seam allowance of the appliqué.

If you are working with slippery fabrics like silks or with small appliqués, it is helpful to baste the seam allowance of the appliqué

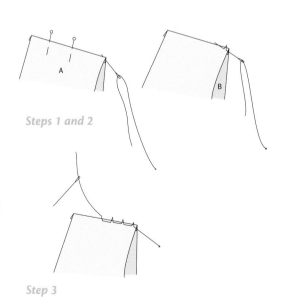

Steps 1 and 2

Step 3

firmly in place before beginning the appliqué stitch. This will prevent distortion of the fabric. Take care to fold over any tips or sharp corners precisely before basting. Remove the basting stitches once the appliqué is in place.

Beading

I have always loved beads and enjoy incorporating them into my sewing. Almost all of the projects in *Thimbles & Things* are embellished with beads. Beading is simple and does not take much time or practice, yet it lends a wonderful new dimension to any decorative project.

Today, there is an incredible variety of beads available from specialty bead stores, catalogs, and web sites. Crafts stores also carry beautiful selections. Because the projects in *Thimbles & Things* are small scale, I tend to choose small beads.

I particularly enjoy highlighting the beautiful patterns I find in fabric with delicate placement of seed beads. My favorites are Japanese delica beads (size 11—the larger the size number, the smaller the bead), which are tiny cylinders, no more than 2 mm long. They come is an amazing variety of colors and finishes. Delicas are easy to sew, lying flat against the fabric and adding texture, dimension, and shine. *Mallow Rose Button Basket* on page 60, is just one of the projects that feature delicas. Tiny daisy patterns made from delicas embellish my otherwise plain thimbles on page 18. I sometimes use Czech seed beads, which have a more rounded shape, in place of delicas. I also like longer cylinder beads, such as 3 mm delicas (size 8). Bugle beads are another favorite. These longer cylinders come in a variety of lengths. *Hagoromo Pincushion* on page 14 features ¾" bugles.

I use small round beads both for sewing directly onto projects, as in *Cherry Needle Cache* on page 56, and, more often, to string onto embroidery floss, then allow them to dangle. Depending on the scale of the project, they may measure anywhere from 3 mm to 6 mm. On occasion, I allow beads to be a focal point of a design and choose beautiful beads, like the one on *Bell Fruit Charms* on page 40. It is fun to spend an hour or two in a specialty store to find beads that will be perfect for your sewing projects. If you do not have a good store in your area, devote a couple of hours to searching beading web sites—and then look forward to your packages of beautiful beads arriving in the mail.

Sewing Beads

While there are specialty threads available from bead stores, designed for sewing beads, I tend to use a strong, high-quality hand-sewing thread or embroidery floss. I use a simple running stitch to sew seed beads or small round beads in place. Sometimes, I follow the design in the fabric or follow the shape of a particular template; other times, I place beads to create distinct patterns, such as the beaded daisies on *Sun Rose Needle Booklet* on page 28. My technique is always the same—a simple running stitch that neatly hides the thread.

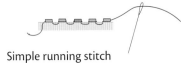

Simple running stitch

Locking beads in place

I secure larger beads by stitching through them two or three times. Sometimes it is necessary to "lock" beads in place, using a small bead or seed bead. I simply stack the desired beads, then run the thread through them as shown. The tiny bead on top locks the others in place. The thread goes through the first and second beads, then through one side of the seed bead and out the other, and back down into the other two beads.

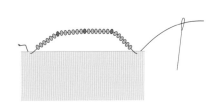

String beads for purse handle

Stringing beads for the handles of projects like *Ivy Heart* on page 32 is easy and fun. Knot a strand of two-ply embroidery floss or heavy-duty sewing thread. Make a stitch to secure it at the spot where the handle starts. String beads in the desired pattern, then make a double stitch at the point where the handle ends.

Materials Needed

Pincushion cover: Cotton scraps in rich florals

Padding: Felt scraps

Stuffing: Batting or fabric scraps

Yo-Yo: Silk or cotton scrap

Beads: 9 small round beads; 6 bugle beads; 12 delica beads

Hagoromo Pincushion

This lovely pincushion doubles as a paperweight. A *hagoromo* is an extremely delicate cloth made of feathers. It is worn by *tennyo*—mythical Japanese ladies who are equivalent to angels in Western culture. *Hagoromo* is also the title of a famous Noh drama, which I remember watching from the front row as a child. The story tells of a *tennyo* who flies from the sky and hangs a beautiful *hagoromo* on a pine branch as she strolls the beach nearby. A fisherman finds it and, fascinated by its unearthly beauty, decides to take it home. The *tennyo*, dismayed at her loss, begs the fisherman to return her treasured cloak to her. He returns it and watches her fly away, her magical *hagoromo* dancing enchantingly behind her. *Hagoromo Pincushion* is much easier to make than it looks and will help you practice several skills: straight sewing, fabric folding, embroidery, and beading. After you've made one for yourself, you'll want to make more for your friends.

羽衣

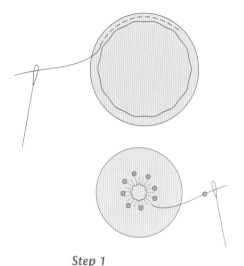

Step 1

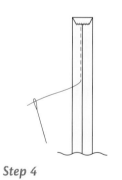

Step 4

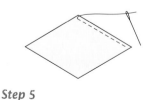

Step 5

Make a yo-yo

1. Cut a circle of fabric measuring 3″ diameter. Fold in the raw edge by about ¼″ and press to hold. Gather stitch around the circumference, through the folded-in seam. Pull the gathers tight and backstitch. Press lightly. Sew decorative beads around the circumference of the yo-yo. (The project photographed uses just six beads, but if your beads are small, you might want to use more.)

Make the pincushion

2. Make a circle template measuring 4¼″ diameter. Cut 3 from felt. Add ¼″ seam allowance to the template (making a 4¾″ circle), then cut one from fabric for the bottom of the pincushion. Cut a strip of felt measuring ¾″ × 12¾″ and a strip of fabric measuring 1¼″ × 13¼″.

3. Fold in a ¼″ seam allowance on the fabric circle from step 2, then press to hold. Slip a felt circle inside the folded-in seam allowance. Sew the felt to the folded-in seam allowance, taking care not to let needle go through to the fabric front. Sew a second circle of felt to the first, hiding the folded-in seam allowance. Trim the second circle slightly.

4. Wrap the felt strip from step 2 inside the fabric strip and sew to hold, as shown.

5. Using diamond template A, cut three. Take care to center any floral pattern on the template. Right sides together, use a running stitch to sew two pieces together along one long edge. Set in the third piece, forming a hexagon out of the three diamonds. Take care to sew neatly from angle to angle. Turn under the remaining raw edges by ¼″. Sew a decorative bead to the center of each diamond.

6. Appliqué the three-piece unit from step 5 onto the remaining circle of felt. Thread a needle with an 18" length of embroidery floss and knot. Inserting from back to front, come up at the outer angle where two diamonds join. Thread a delica, a bugle bead, and a second delica, allowing them to lie along the edge of the pieced diamond. Make a stitch into the felt to secure. Come up again about 1" away, and thread a second set of delica-bugle-delica, this time securing at the next outer angle. Repeat around the perimeter of the pieced diamonds, securing a total of six bead sets (two per diamond).

7. Pin a long edge of the fabric-covered felt strip from step 4 evenly around the circumference of the pincushion top from step 6. Use a two-ply strand of embroidery floss and herringbone stitch to attach the strip, removing pins as you go. When the two ends of the strip meet, use overcast stitch to sew them together. Repeat, this time sewing the remaining long edge of the strip to the pincushion base. Before closing, stuff firmly with batting or cotton scraps.

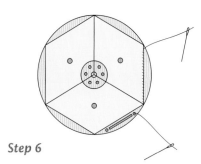

Step 6

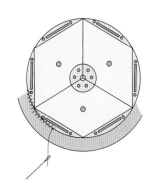

Step 7

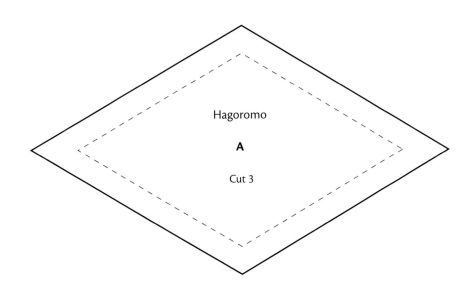

Hagoromo

A

Cut 3

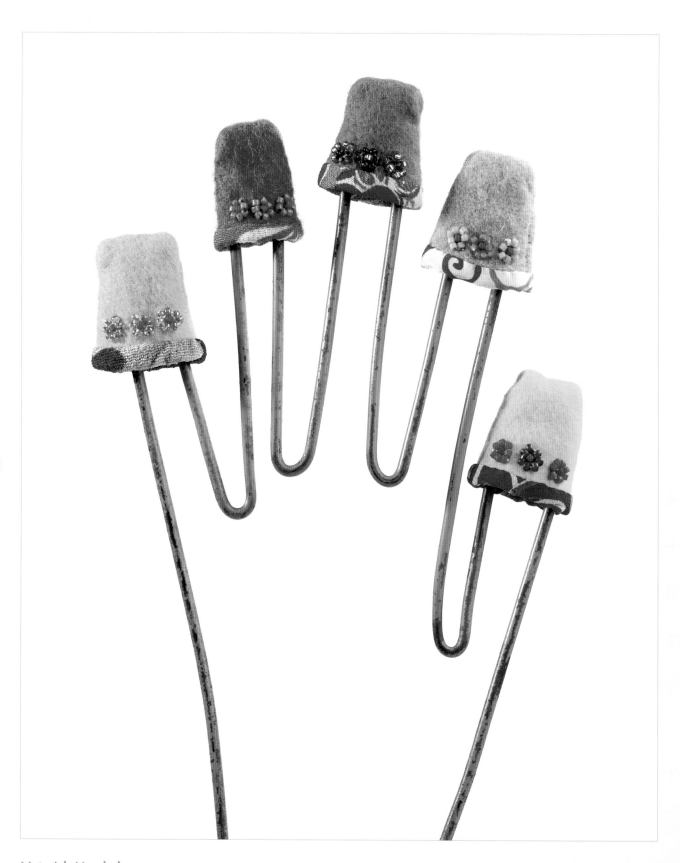

Materials Needed

Thimble: **Felt scraps**

Trim: **Cotton or silk scraps for trim**

Beads: **21 delica beads per thimble**

Nimble Thimbles

These pretty thimbles will protect your fingers while adding a splash of color to your sewing box. They are made from a double layer of felt, and can be embellished any way you wish. I used bright colors so that I can easily find a thimble when I need one! Keep a few in your sewing room, more in your sew-and-go bag.

Fabric thimbles make great gifts for children, too. Better still, combine your gift with a quick sewing lesson by giving one completed thimble and the makings for a second. Little projects like this are a very good introduction to sewing for young children.

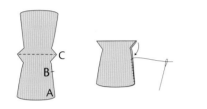

Step 1

Step 2

Step 3

Make a thimble

1. Using template A, cut a thimble from felt. Fold the piece in half along the dotted line, as shown. Using overcast stitch, sew from A to B, securing at B with a double stitch.

2. Push from the base to create a y shape as shown, and sew both short seams. Turn right side out.

3. Cut a strip of fabric measuring ¾" × 3". Position it right sides around the top edge of the thimble. Using an ⅛" seam allowance, sew the trim in place around the circumference of the thimble. Open out the seam. Turn the other long edge and the short ends inwards by 1/8" and press to hold. Appliqué in place around the inside circumference of the thimble.

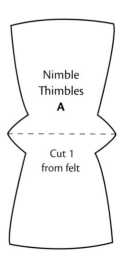

Nimble
Thimbles
A

Cut 1
from felt

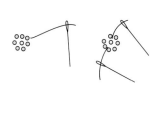

Complete

4. Make three beaded daisies, as shown. First, sew the center bead in place, then string and sew six beads evenly around it. See page 13 for help with sewing beads.

Thimbles make such lovely little gifts and looking for creative ways to wrap them makes them all the more welcome. In the photograph, I popped the thimbles inside a box of traditional Japanese tea candy to make it feel special.

Step 4

Materials Needed

Flower fabrics: ¼ yd each or scraps of at least five fabrics

Handles: ⅛ yd or scraps of each of two fabrics

12 decorative pearls, beads, or buttons

Sun Rose Sewing Box

Let this delightful flower box bring the zest of Spring into your home. It makes a lovely sewing kit, prettily accommodating scissors, threads, a thimble, and fabric scraps—there's even a needle case to match! Take the kit along with you to view cherry trees in bloom as you quietly stitch in a shower of falling petals. If you make *Sun Rose Sewing Box* for someone who doesn't sew, notice that it is the perfect size to neatly disguise a small box of tissues!

Each of the square sides of *Sun Rose Sewing Box* is created using a fabric origami technique, where a fabric circle is folded to create a square shape. A key difference between folding paper and folding fabric is that paper is available with different colors on the two sides. To achieve the same effect with fabric, you must first sew the two colors of your choice together, then turn them right side out and press. Often, finger pressing will be adequate.

Make double-sided circles

1. Choose two complementary fabrics, taking care to achieve good color contrast. From each, cut 12 circles measuring 8½" in diameter.

2. Matching contrasting colors (light to dark) and right sides together, sew the pairs together by hand or by machine around the outer edges, leaving a 2" opening. Use ¼" seam allowance.

3. Fold the seams inward toward the center of the circle and press. Follow the curved line to make a nice, rounded curve. Turn the shape right side out, then blind-stitch the opening closed. Lightly press to reinforce the shape.

Repeat Steps 1 to 3 until you have have made 12 double-sided circles. I recommend mixing up fabrics in the same color family, making four sets of three identical circles. You are free to make as many different combinations as you choose.

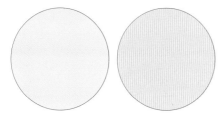

Step 2

Step 3

Step 4

Make twelve flowers

4. Lightly fold each circle horizontally then vertically to find center. Mark center lightly on both sides.

5. Fold each side inward by 1" at its midpoint to create a square. Pin in place.

6. Turn over. Fold all corners to center point of square. Make one or two small stitches to secure tip of each corner in place. Press.

Join the flowers

7. Lay out completed flowers in rows of three as shown and in a manner that pleases you. Note that flowers 3, 6, 9, and 12 form bottom of box. As photographed, these flowers are made from the same two fabrics. Pin a number to each flower so that you sew in correct sequence.

8. Pick up flowers 1 and 2. With right sides together, connect along one side using fine coil stitch (see next page). In same way, add flower 3.

9. Complete four sets of three flowers.

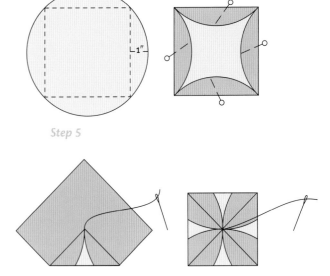

Step 5

Step 6

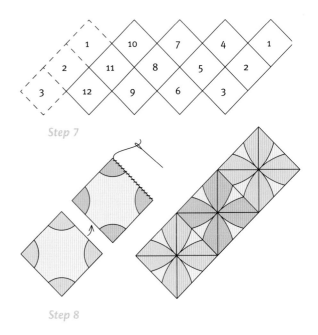

Step 7

Step 8

Coil Stitch

This easy-to-learn technique allows you to connect the flowers together without puckers and with fine, even stitches. Pin two flowers right sides together, aligning the edges. Knot your thread and begin with a double stitch. Taking one stitch at a time and moving from right to left, insert the needle at a 45° angle through the front fabric facing you. Push through all layers and exit the needle at the back of the work, ⅛" or less to the left of your entry point. Tug the thread then loop over the top of the work to take your next stitch. When you reach the end of your row of stitches, take three backstitches to secure. The line of stitches on the back side of your work will be on the diagonal; the stitches at the front will be near-invisible and recessed into the fabric.

Coil stitch—begin with backstitch

Work from right to left

End with backstitches

Diagonal stitches on the back side

Near invisible stitches on the front side

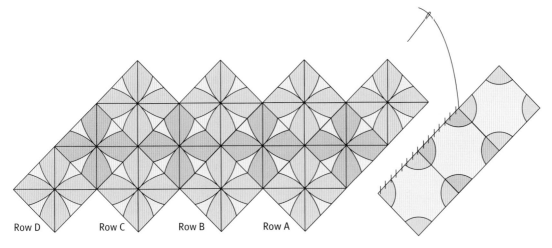

Row D   Row C   Row B   Row A

Step 11

10. Using coil stitches and wrong sides together, connect four rows, offsetting each by one flower as shown.

11. To make box bottom, use coil stitch, right sides together, to connect bottom edge of flower 3 in row A to right edge of flower 6 in row B. In same way, sew bottom edge of flower 6 to right edge of flower 9 in row C; sew bottom edge of flower 9 to right edge of flower 12 in row D; sew bottom edge of flower 12 to right edge of flower 3 in row A. The box bottom is magically complete! Turn right side out. If you wish, press lightly to reinforce shape.

12. Stitch decorative bead or pearl to center of each flower, except those on bottom. Stitch another at every point at which four flowers meet, as shown in photograph.

13. Using template A and adding ¼" seam allowance, cut two handle pieces from each of two complementary fabrics. Matching different fabrics and right sides together, stitch around all edges, leaving 2" opening. Turn right side out and press lightly to reinforce curves at either end. Repeat for second handle. Sew one curved end to wrong side of each of four flower tips at top of box.

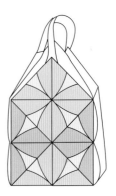

Step 13

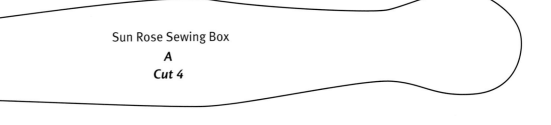

Sun Rose Sewing Box
A
Cut 4

Materials Needed

Flower fabrics: ⅛ yd or scraps of two fabrics

Felt in two colors: **Piece A is 3 ¼ x 8"; piece B is 3 ¾" x 7 ¾"**

¼" ribbon: **14"**

2 decorative pearls

Decorative beads to embellish spine

Small thread scissors (optional)

Sun Rose Needle Case

This little needle case using the same design as *Sun Rose Sewing Box*. Together, they make a lovely companion set. The cover of the booklet is made from two *Sun Rose* flowers, connected by a strip of felt.

My booklet is made of felt, but you can experiment and use the *Sun Rose* cover for anything you wish. Slip a photo inside the back of one of the flowers and you have an instant photo frame, for instance.

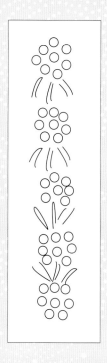

8"

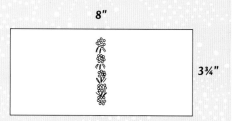

3¾"

Center flower is created from 7 tiny green seed beads and one yellow bead. Stems of other four flowers are made from ¼" cylindrical beads.

Detail, beaded flower

Beaded Flowers

Make these tiny flowers from small beads. Sew the center bead to the felt, exiting the needle on the right side. Using a complimentary color, string seven beads, allowing them to wrap around the center bead. Draw the needle back through to the wrong side of the felt, then make two small stitches at either side of the circle to hold the beads in place. Stitch ¼" cylindrical beads in place to create stems and leaves.

Make two flowers

1. Follow step 1 to 6 of *Sun Rose Sewing Box* on page 24 to make two flowers.

2. Sew decorative beads as desired or as shown down center of larger piece of felt, piece A. Center flower is created from 7 tiny green seed beads and one yellow bead. Stems of other four flowers are made from. cylindrical beads.

3. Position smaller piece of felt, piece B, on top of first. Make single line of running stitch down center to hold two pieces together.

4. Position completed flowers on either side of beaded spine. Spine should measure about ½" wide. Pin to hold in place. With felt side facing you, stitch flowers in place along spine edge only.

Add ribbon

5. Loop one end of ribbon through one of finger holes in scissors. Fold ribbon over by about ½" and stitch edges to hold scissors securely in place. Fold other end of ribbon over by about 2" and stitch in place onto felt as shown, leaving ¾" of loop free.

6. If necessary, trim back felt so that it does not show when booklet is closed.

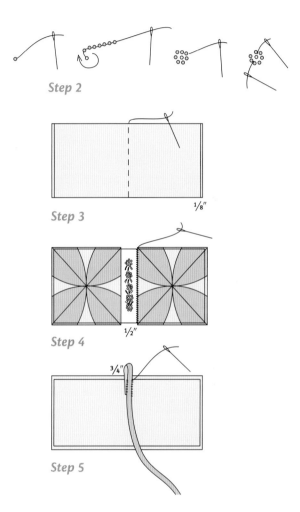

Step 2

Step 3
⅛"

Step 4
½"

Step 5
¾"

Materials Needed

Pocket: fabric and felts in similar tones

Yo-yo: scraps of silk or cotton

Beads: mixture of small beads, bugle beads, and seed beads

Embroidery floss

Ivy Heart

Ivy Heart is a simple gift to make by hand and give with all your heart. Imagine a mother's delight when she opens a package on Valentine's Day or Mother's Day to find this lovely thread and pin tote inside. It will hang prettily over a chair arm and take care of her needle and pins as she sews.

Pocket

1. With template A, cut eight hearts from felt. Add ¼" seam allowance then cut four from fabric. Fold in seam allowances on each fabric piece and press to hold. Slip a felt piece inside folded-in seam allowance of its corresponding fabric piece. Sew felt to folded-in seam allowance, taking care not to let needle go through to pocket front. Trim remaining felt pieces to make them ¹⁄₁₆" or less smaller than others. Position one on top of each felt-backed piece, felt sides touching, then sew in place. Make four.

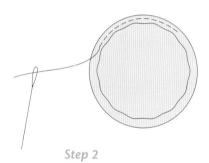

Step 2

Step 3

2. Cut a circle from cotton or silk, measuring 2¾" in diameter. Fold in raw edge by about ⅛" and press to hold. Gather stitch around circumference. Pull gathers tight and backstitch. Press lightly. Fold yo-yo just above center, so that front half is slightly larger than back half. Position about ½" from top center at front of one of hearts, then stitch in place.

3. Cut two small circles from felt (about ⅞" and ⅝" in diameter). Sew together, attaching a circle of seed beads at same time. Sew more beads to center of circles as desired. Sew in place on top of yo-yo. Add more beads as desired to this pocket front.

4. Cut two strips of felt measuring ⅜" × 9½" Place one on top of other, then stitch together. Join ends to make loop. Pin one edge of loop around heart from Step 2, then stitch in place. Stitch another felt-backed heart shape to other edge of loop. Use a simple overstitch or coil stitch (see page 26). This forms pincushion around perimeter of heart.

5. Use embroidery floss and herringbone stitch to sew remaining two heart shapes together, stopping at points A and leaving top open as shown. Add beads to front of heart shape as desired.

6. String beads as desired to a length of about 6½". Sew ends of bead-string to inside of each heart pocket.

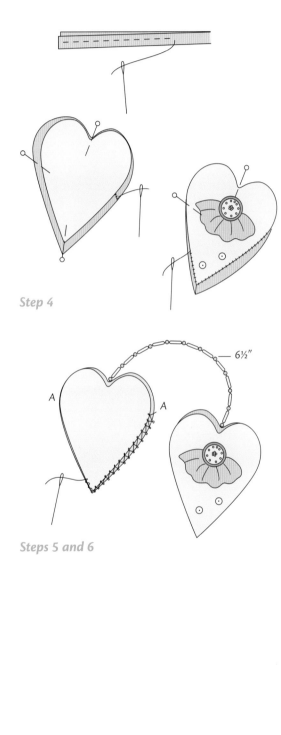

Step 4

Steps 5 and 6

Ivy Pocket
A

*Cut 4 from fabric
(add ¼" seam allowance)*

Cut 8 from felt

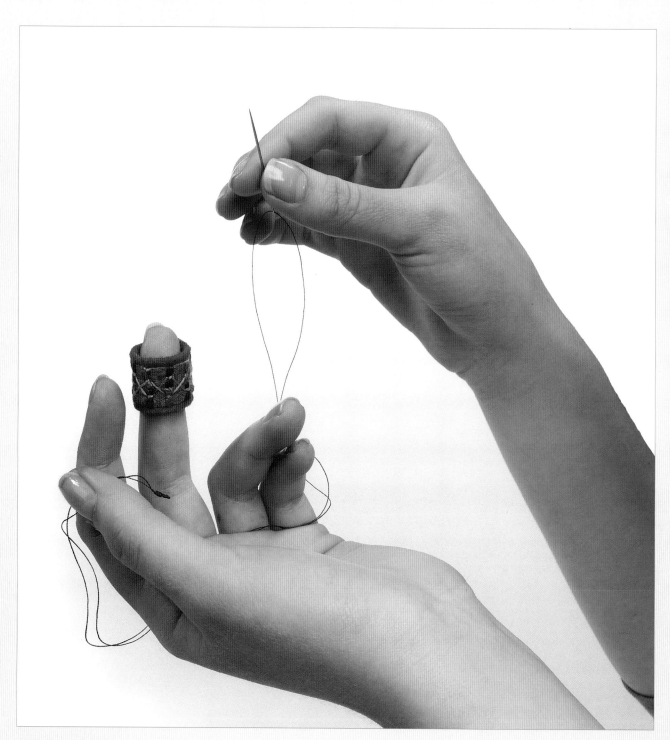

Materials Needed

Fabrics: Silk or cotton scraps; felt scraps

Embroidery floss: 2-ply in multiple colors

Embroidered Thimbles!

I like the softness of traditional Japanese thimbles made from fabric. I also find that my thimble finger does not tire as easily as it might with a metal thimble. I love to make these pretty little rings and use them to hold notes or gift tags, as well as for sewing! You might even want to wear them as jewelry for your fingers or toes! I've suggested four embroidery patterns, but you will soon want to create a design of your own.

Thimble

Cut a strip of felt measuring ½" × 2¼" and a strip of fabric measuring 1" × 2¾". Test length of felt strip around your finger and adjust size as necessary. Fold in all sides of fabric strip by ¼" and press. Position on top of felt strip, then use small overstitch to sew in place. Draw guidelines to create grid, shown in red in diagrams. Begin embroidery design. Where possible, try to hide back stitches between fabric and felt—there is no need to stitch all way through felt. When embroidery is complete, join ends to make a loop, adjusting size as necessary.

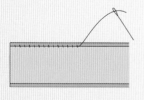 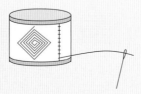

Design A

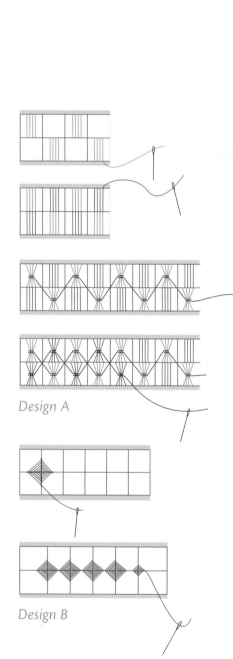

Design A

Design B

Design A

With first floss color, make four large stitches from top to bottom of every second grid square as shown. Repeat in alternate grid squares, using second floss color. With third floss color, make a double stitch at center of first set of four threads, grouping threads together to create haystack shape. Cross diagonally. Continue along length of thimble to next set of four threads and repeat.

Design B

Beginning at first point where guidelines cross, embroider a tiny square. Make up to six more squares around this one, each larger than the previous. If desired, switch colors for the final two squares. Repeat along length of fabric.

Design B

Design C

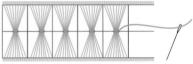

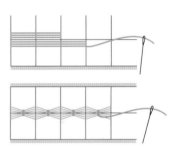

Design C

Make large stitches from to bottom of fabric as shown.
You will need about ten stitches to fill each grid division.
Changing floss color, make a double stitch at center of first
set of threads (between grid lines), grouping threads together
to create haystack shape. Cross to next set of four threads
and repeat. Continue along length of thimble.

Design C

Design D

Make five large stitches across width of each grid square as
shown. (If desired, use two different colors of floss.) Change
colors, then make a double stitch at center of first set of
threads, grouping threads together to create horizontal
haystack shape. Cross to next set of four threads and repeat.
Continue along length of thimble.

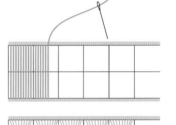

Design D

Design D

Materials Needed

Berry: **Scraps**

Yo-yos: **Silk scraps**

Stuffing: **Batting or fabric scraps**

⅛" ribbon: **10"**

Bell Fruit Charms

These tiny charms are inspired by memories of the soft handballs my mother would make for me as a child. Use them as you please on gift wrap, or as lamp pulls, key rings, or scissor fobs. The choice—and the daily pleasure they give—is yours. I like to add little touches like this to every gift I send. Long after the candy in the box is gone, your friends will enjoy this elegant hand-made gift tie.

Can there be any better way to use up tiny scraps of fabric? If I love a fabric for its pattern, texture, or sheen, I have a difficult time throwing away even the smallest pieces. This little project will put those scraps to good use. It is also an interesting way to experiment with color. Take special care to choose ribbons and beads that will compliment your fabric choices!

果物可愛い

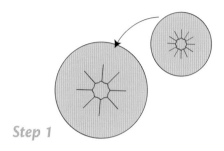

Step 1

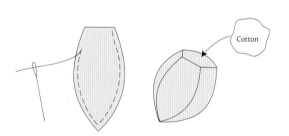

Cotton

Step 2

Make a double yo-yo

1. Cut one circle measuring 2" and another measuring 2 ¼" in diameter. Fold in the raw edges by about ⅛" and press to hold. Gather stitch around the circumference, through the folded-in seam. Pull the gathers tight and backstitch. Press lightly. Make one or two stitches at the center to secure the smaller yo-yo on, top of the larger one.

Make the berry

2. With template A, cut five from fabric. Using a ⅛" seam allowance, sew the five pieces together lengthwise to form the berry shape, leaving the top open. Fold the top seam allowance inwards and finger-press to hold. Stuff firmly with cotton batting or fabric scraps.

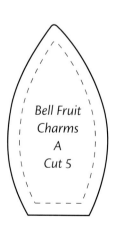

Bell Fruit
Charms
A
Cut 5

3. Gather-stitch around the top of the berry, through the folded in seam allowance. Pull the gathers tight, trapping the batting inside, then stitch to secure. Do not cut the thread yet.

Complete

4. Use the same thread to stitch the double yo-yo on top of the berry.

5. Make a small knot at either end of the ribbon, then fold it in half. Stuff the knots inside the top-most yo-yo and stitch to secure.

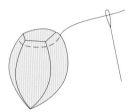

Step 3

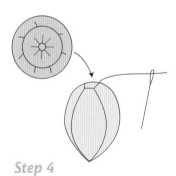

Step 4

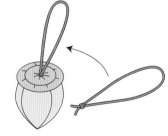

Step 5

Materials Needed

Fabrics: combination of up to three silks or cottons for outside; felt in up to four colors for lining

Beads: about 350 seed beads

Embroidery floss in multiple colors (up to six)

Stuffing

Heian Pin & Thimble Box

This design is inspired by the Heian period in Japanese antiquity (794 to 1185), when the achievement of elegance in arts and crafts was a reflection of life in the Imperial Court. Ladies sought to surround themselves with beauty and every item they used combined elegance with practicality.

This decorative sewing case beautifully combines a soft pincushion with a hide-away for threads, needles, and other small accessories. The colorful embroidery around the sides, as well as the delicate seed beads, add a sophisticated touch. Use ¼" seam allowance for sewing.

Embroidered Bands

1. Cut four strips measuring ¾" × 9½" from felt; cut two from fabric. Fold in seam allowances on fabric pieces by a scant ⅛" on all sides and press to hold. Position each on top of a corresponding felt piece, then use tiny stitches and matching thread to sew in place. About ⅛" of felt will show behind fabric. Make two.

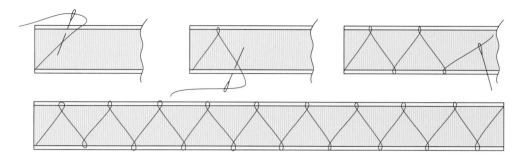

Step 2

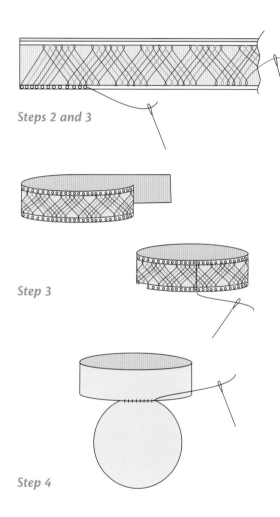

Steps 2 and 3

Step 3

Step 4

2. With chalk or other marker, make guide points every inch along top and bottom edges. With two-ply embroidery floss and herringbone stitch, stitch as shown, going from guide points at bottom edge to top edge as shown. For small, neat herringbone stitches, begin by entering from back and hiding knot on back side of band. Exiting at front bottom, draw thread upwards and diagonally to right, then make a small stitch at top, as shown. Needle exits immediately to left of its entry point. Draw thread downwards and diagonally to right, then make a tiny stitch at bottom. Continue to end of band. Change to another color thread, then repeat, beginning about ⅛" away from first set of stitches. Repeat for a total of six sets.

3. Sew seed beads in place onto felt above and below fabric strip. Position on top of remaining strip of felt, with felt sides touching. Pin, then sew together. For embroidered band on box lid in photograph, allow ⅛" of this new felt piece (green) to show behind first felt piece (yellow). For bottom embroidered band, trim felt (purple) so that it is exactly even with first felt piece (red). Sew ends together to make loop.

Base

4. Cut three 3" diameter circles from felt; cut three 3½" diameter circles from fabric. Fold in ¼" seam allowances on each fabric piece and press to hold. Slip a corresponding felt piece inside folded-in seam allowance of fabric pieces. Set one completed circle aside for top. Sew one completed circle to base of bottom embroidered band as shown. Use a simple overstitch or coil stitch (see page 26). Slip remaining circle inside band and make stitches at 1" intervals around perimeter to attach to base.

Top

5. Using remaining felt-backed circle from Step 4, overstitch or coil stitch in place around remaining embroidered band to form base of top. Cut 6" diameter circle from fabric. Pin or baste in place around perimeter of embroidered band. Take out one or two pins, then stuff as full as possible with stuffing, achieving as soft, rounded shape. Sew fabric carefully in place, manipulating shape as you go and stitching through overhanging edge of felt (green in photograph) at top of embroidered band.

6. Cut a 2" square of fabric. Fold all four sides inwards by about ¼" and press. Fold in half, then sew around edges as shown. Position then stitch onto top and base as shown.

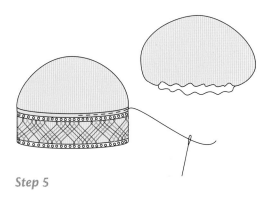

Step 5

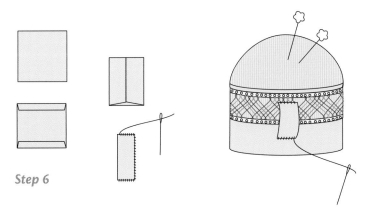

Step 6

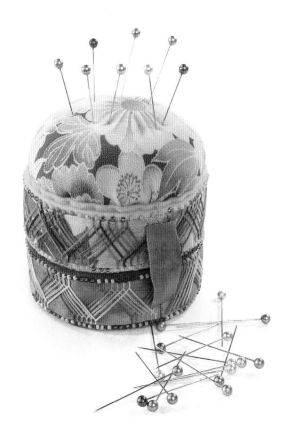

Materials Needed

Pincushion: cotton or silk; felt in contrast color for calyx

Leaf: fabric scrap

Beads: about 50 seed beads

Cotton stuffing or batting scraps

Persimmon Pincushion

Everyone who sews needs a variety of pincushions! The pretty persimmon shape is easy to make and is small enough to carry along in your sewing kit.

For friends who do not sew, it's easy to make the same design as a paperweight. To add weight, stuff with beans or rice, or, for a softer feel, stuff with a mixture of rice and batting.

Pincushion

1. Cut circle measuring 6 ½" in diameter from fabric. Take a running stitch around circumference, stuff with batting, and pull gathering stitches. Stuff until pincushion is very firm. Pull gathers tight and backstitch to hold.

2. Using template A, cut two from felt for calyx. Sew together around perimeter, adding seed beads as you stitch.

3. Cut strip of felt measuring ½" × 1 ½" for short stem. Roll lengthwise and stitch to hold. Repeat with 1 ½" square of felt for longer stem. Place longer stem across top of shorter stem and stitch in place. Stitch to calyx, then stitch calyx to top of pincushion.

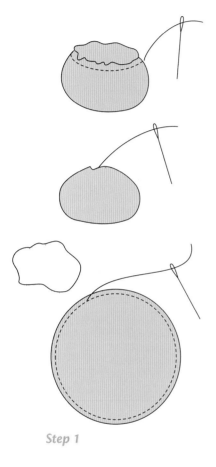

Step 1

Step 2

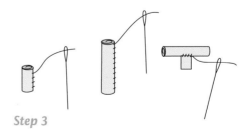

Step 3

4. With template B, cut two from fabric for leaf. Right sides together, stitch around perimeter, leaving about 1" open. Turn right side out. then blind stitch opening closed. To make leaf veins, fold leaf in half lengthwise, then sew very close to folded edge (¹⁄₁₆" or less). Open out, then carefully fold along dashed lines of template. Again, stitch very close to edge.

5. Sew tip of leaf in place at center of calyx.

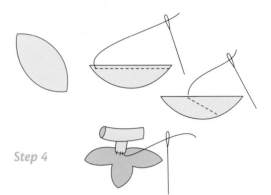

Step 4

Step 5

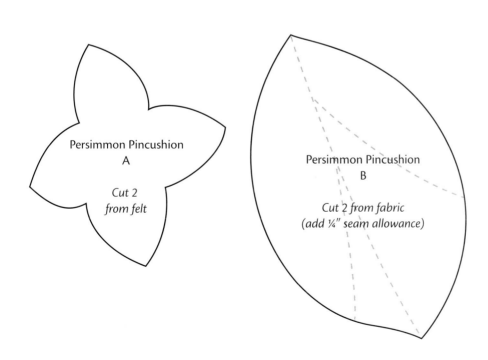

Persimmon Pincushion
A

*Cut 2
from felt*

Persimmon Pincushion
B

*Cut 2 from fabric
(add ¼" seam allowance)*

Materials Needed

Tote: decorative cotton; felt in matching color

Flower: silk scraps

Beads: about 40 small beads; large decorative bead or combination of one large, one small, and one seed bead; about 50 seed beads for interior

Cotton stuffing or batting scraps

Embroidery floss

Two snap fasteners

Tidy Tote

Sweet and pretty, this little tote will keep your needles, threads, and pins in place from the beginning to the end of a sewing project. Open it up and you'll find a handy pincushion sewn into the base of the tote—no more loose pins, even when you sew on-the-go.

Step 1

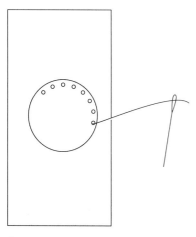

Step 3

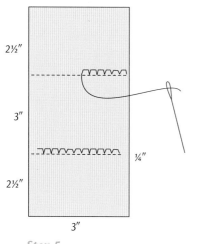

2½"

3"

2½"

¼"

3"

Step 5

Buds

1. Cut three circles measuring 1⅔" from a wide silk ribbon or from silk or cotton. Fold in half, then fold inwards from either side as shown. Gather stitch along top, then pull gathers gently to create petal shape. Stitch to hold. Make three.

Tote

2. Cut strip of fabric measuring 4½" × 8½" cut two strips of felt measuring 4" × 8" With template A, cut four from felt; add ¼" seam allowance then cut two from fabric. Fold in ¼" seam allowances on each fabric piece and press to hold. Slip a felt piece inside folded-in seam allowance of its corresponding fabric piece. Sew felt to folded-in seam allowance, taking care not to let needle go through to tote front.

3. Cut a 2½" diameter circle from felt. Position at center of remaining felt strip. Sew seed beads in place, stitching through both layers of felt. When about 1" remains unstitched, stuff tightly with batting to form pincushion. Complete stitching of beads.

4. Position felt strip with pincushion on top of felt-backed fabric strip, with felts next to each other. Pin in place. Stitch around entire perimeter, stitching through felt layers only. Make sure your stitches do not come through to the front.

5. At dashed lines, pinch about ⅛" fabric only (not felt lining) and, using embroidery floss, blanket-stitch along width of tote, starting and stopping about ¼" from either end.

6. Position remaining template A pieces on top of felt-backed template A pieces, with felts next to each other. Pin, then use a small overstitch to sew around both pieces, taking care not to allow needle to go through to tote front. Use blanket stitch and embroidery floss to sew sides of tote in place. Sew snap fasteners at top inside corners of tote, stitching through felt only.

Complete

7. Position buds from Step 1 at center front of tote, then sew in place. Attach large bead as in photograph, locking it in place with a small bead and a seed bead. Knot thread and bring from inside to front of tote, immediately to right of right-most bud. String beads onto thread as desired for about 4", then draw thread from tote front to inside and backstitch to hold. Make another 1" string of beads and secure one end of it beneath button.

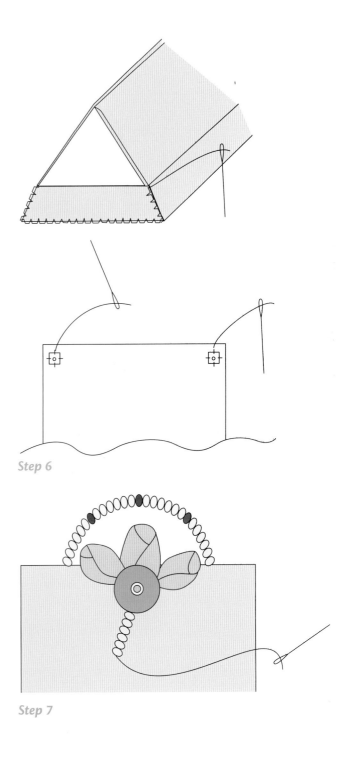

Step 6

Step 7

Tidy
Tote
A

*Cut 2
from fabric
(add ¼"
seam
allowance)*

*Cut 4
from felt*

Materials Needed

Booklet: silk or cotton; felt in contrast color

Buds: silk, cotton, or felt scraps; silk or cotton scraps for stems and hanging loop

Beads: about 150 seed beads

Cotton stuffing or batting scraps

Cherry Booklet

Keep you pins safe and your needles organized by size in this leaf-shaped booklet. Hang it in your sewing area and you will always be able to find fresh needles and pins when you need them.

Of course, the little beaded balls have many embellishment possibilities. Use them to create little charms to wrap around the stems of wine glasses, so your guests always know which glass is theirs.

Booklet

1. With template A, cut seven from felt. Add ½" seam allowance, then cut two from fabric. Fold in seam allowances on each fabric piece and press to hold. Slip a felt piece inside folded-in seam allowance of each fabric piece. Sew felt to folded-in seam allowance, taking care not to let needle go through to front. Sew another felt piece on top, hiding fabric seam allowance. (If necessary, trim felt piece so that it is about ⅛" smaller than felt-backed fabric.) Make two.

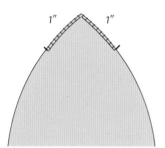

1"   1"

Step 2

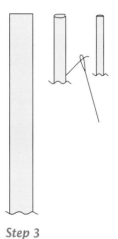

Step 3

2. Place remaining three felt pieces between booklet covers. Using embroidery floss and buttonhole stitch, sew through all layers for about 1" along either side of tip.

Cherries

3. To make stems, cut three strips measuring ½" × 7", one strip measuring ½" × 5", and three strips measuring ½" × 3½" Fold in half and sew edges together lengthwise, using scant ⅛" seam allowance. Turn right side out.

4. Cut four 2" diameter circles from fabric and five from felt. Gather stitch around perimeter. Stuff with batting then pull gathers to create ball shape. Stuff one end of each stem into gathers, then backstitch to hold. Repeat, stuffing other end of longer stems into another cherry. Four stems will now have cherries attached at either end; shortest stem will have a cherry at one end. As desired, sew seed beads to some of cherries

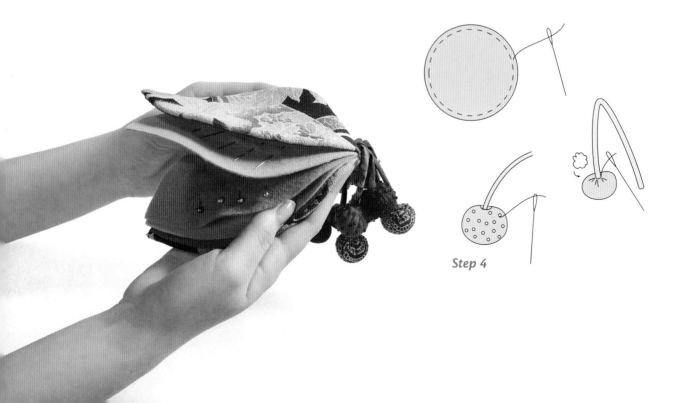

Step 4

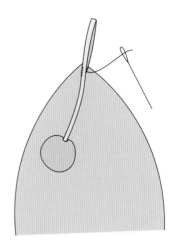

5. Make a loop at top of shortest stem by folding end without cherry over by about ¾" and sewing in place to center of stem. Without cutting thread, sew to tip of front cover of booklet. Fold stems of remaining cherries in half, then sew this center point in place at tip, adjusting lengths of stems as desired.

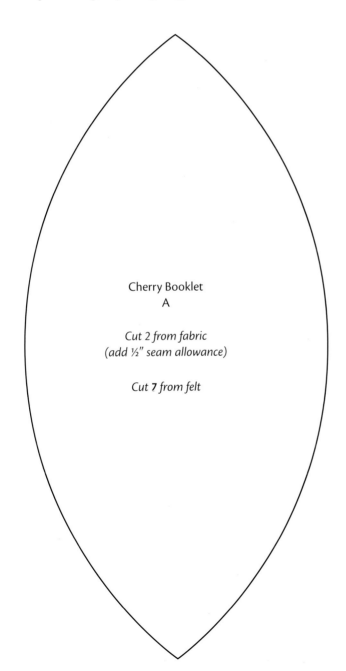

Cherry Booklet
A

Cut 2 from fabric
(add ½" seam allowance)

*Cut **7** from felt*

Step 5

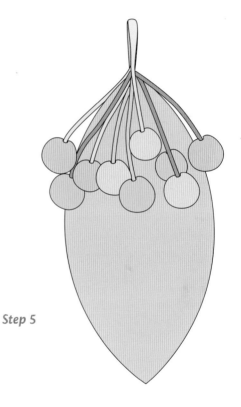

Materials Needed

Bowl: cotton or silk; felt in contrast color

Pincushion: silk and felt scraps

Beads: about 600 seed beads

Cotton stuffing or batting scraps

Mallow Rose Button Basket

Designed to hold a simple round pincushion, you can use this little fabric bowl for anything you please. I like to use mine to keep any buttons or beads I am using for a project or that I am saving for something special. It makes a pretty candy dish or it can hold a favorite piece of jewelry while brightening up your dresser.

Notice how I have used little delica beads to emphasise the pattern that already exists in the fabric. You can do the same. Or instead, if you choose a fabric that has no distinct pattern, you can use delica beads to create a design of your own. You can also brighten up your fabric through the colors you choose for the beading.

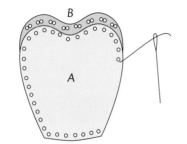

Step 1

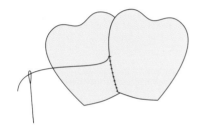

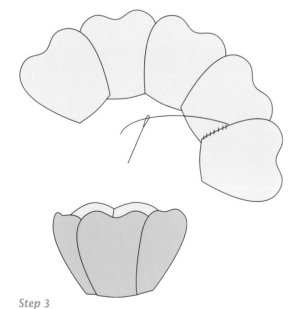

Step 3

Bowl

1. With template A, cut five from felt; add ½" seam allowance and cut five from fabric. Fold in seam allowances on each fabric piece and press to hold. Slip a corresponding felt piece inside folded-in seam allowance. Sew felt to folded-in seam allowance, taking care not to let needle go through to front. Make five.

2. With template B, cut five from felt. Position a fabric-wrapped shape from Step 1 on top of each. Sew together as you stitch beads in place. Sew additional beads at top of B pieces.

3. Overlapping by about ¼" stitch two completed leaves together, starting at base and stitching for about 1". Repeat until all five leaves are connected, then stitch last leaf to first in same way.

4. With template C, cut one from felt. Overstitch to bottom of flower piece to create bowl.

Pincushion

5. Cut a 4" diameter circle from fabric and a ¾" circle from felt. Gather stitch around perimeter of fabric circle. Stuff with batting then pull gathers to create ball shape. Backstitch to hold. Sew felt circle in place, hiding gathers.

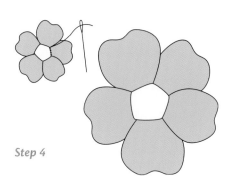

Step 4

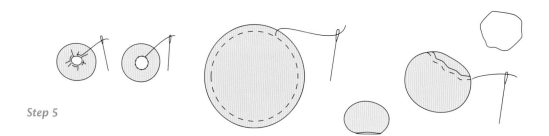

Step 5

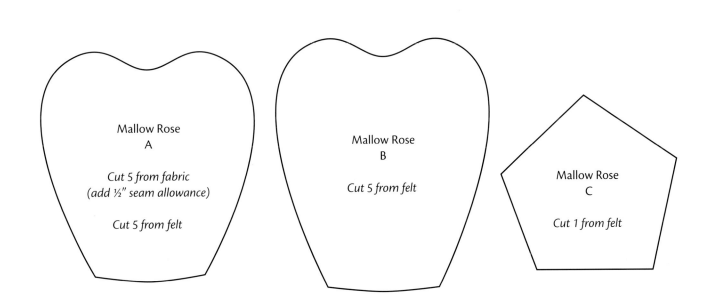

Mallow Rose
A

*Cut 5 from fabric
(add ½" seam allowance)*

Cut 5 from felt

Mallow Rose
B

Cut 5 from felt

Mallow Rose
C

Cut 1 from felt

Resources

The many unusual Japanese supplies used in these projects are part of what makes them so fun. Be sure to check first with your local shops for unique fabrics, cords, threads, and embellishments, but if you are unable to find them in your area, the following on-line retailers and importers are great resources:

Fabric

In the Beginning Fabrics
www.inthebeginningfabrics.com
800-523-1001
(for wholesale orders only)

Quilters' Express to Japan
www.qejapan.com
570-522-7480

Hoffman Fabrics
www.hoffmanfabrics.com
800-547-0100

Ah! Kimono
www.ahkimono.com
425-482-6485

Bali Farics
www.balifab.com
800-783-4612

Beads & Buttons

Ah! Kimono
www.ahkimono.com
425-482-6485

Artbeads.com
www.artbeads.com

Fire Mountain Gems and Beads
www.firemountaingems.com
800-355-2137

Cord

Fire Mountain Gems and Beads
www.firemountaingems.com
800-355-2137

Felt

National Nonwovens
800-333-3469
www.nationalnonwovens.com

Thread

Clover NeedlecraftInc.
www.clover-use.com

DMC
www.dmc-usa.com
973-589-0606

Sulky
www.sulky.com
800-874-4115

YLI Thread
www.ylicorp.com
803-985-3100

Notions

Clover Needlecraft Inc.
www.clover-usa.com

Books

Breckling Press
www.brecklingpress.com
630-941-1179